The Brain-Co... Interface Revolution

Applications, Ethics, and the Future of Humanity

Benjamin Evans

DEDICATION

To the relentless seekers of knowledge, the curious minds tirelessly decoding the mysteries of algorithms and code. This book is dedicated to you, the coders who embrace the challenges of neural networks with fervor and determination. May these pages serve as stepping stones on your journey, empowering you to unravel the complexities of this dynamic field and craft solutions that shape the future. Your passion fuels the innovation that drives our world forward, and for that, I extend my deepest gratitude and admiration.

CONTENTS

ACKNOWLEDGMENTS..1

CHAPTER 1...1

Unveiling the Mysterious Mind......................................1

1.1 A Brief History of Brain Exploration: From Ancient Egypt to Modern Neuroscience.. 1

1.2 The Language of the Brain: Decoding Neurons and Neural Networks...5

1.3 Mapping the Mind: Exploring the Functional Areas of the Brain 8

1.4 The Limits of the Human Brain: Understanding Our Cognitive Constraints..11

CHAPTER 2... 15

Birth of the Brain-Computer Interface (BCI): A Technological Revolution15

2.1 From Science Fiction to Reality: The Early Dreams of BCI Technology..15

2.2 Non-invasive vs. Invasive BCIs: Weighing the Risks and Rewards 17

2.3 How Does a BCI Work? Translating Brain Signals into Actionable Commands...19

2.4 The Future of BCI Design: Addressing Challenges and Pushing the Boundaries... 21

CHAPTER 3... 25

BCIs for Healthcare: Restoring Function and Enhancing Lives.................25

3.1 Aiding Individuals with Paralysis: Regaining Control Through Thought-Controlled Devices......................... 25

3.2 Communication Regained: Empowering People with Speech Loss to Express Themselves........................... 28

3.3 Beyond Physical Limitations: Exploring BCIs for Mental Health Treatment....................................... 31

3.4 The Ethical Landscape of Neurorehabilitation: Balancing Benefits with Patient Autonomy.......................33

CHAPTER 4... 36

BCIs for Augmentation: Redefining Human Potential..........................**36**

4.1 Beyond Human Limits: Enhancing Sensory Perception and Cognitive Abilities.. 36

4.2 The Rise of the Cyborg: Merging Human and Machine Intelligence... 38

4.3 Brain-Computer Interfaces in Education: Personalized Learning and Knowledge Augmentation...................................... 41

4.4 Ethical Considerations of Human Enhancement: Ensuring Equity and Preventing Abuse...43

4.5 Conclusion: A Future of Human Potential, Amplified............ 45

CHAPTER 5... **47**

BCIs in Gaming and Entertainment: Blurring the Lines Between Reality and Fantasy.. **47**

5.1 The Future of Gaming: Immersive Experiences Controlled by Your Thoughts...47

5.2 Beyond Entertainment: BCIs for Art, Music, and Creative Expression...50

5.3 The Challenges of Brain-Computer Interaction: Ensuring User Experience and Security.. 51

5.4 The Ethical Debate: Blurring the Lines Between Player and Character.. 52

CHAPTER 6... **56**

BCIs in Communication: Revolutionizing How We Interact with the World 56

6.1 Thought-Controlled Communication: From Telepathy to Direct Brain-to-Brain Interaction..56

6.2 The Future of Social Media: Sharing Thoughts and Emotions Directly...60

6.3 Language Learning Reimagined: Accelerated Learning Through Brain-Computer Interfaces... 61

6.4 The Power of Empathy: Fostering Deeper Understanding Through Shared Brain Activity.. 63

CHAPTER 7... **67**

BCIs in the Workplace: Transforming How We Work and Learn............ **67**

7.1 Increased Productivity and Efficiency: Enhancing Cognitive Performance in the Workplace...67

7.2 Brain-Computer Training: Optimizing Skill Development and Problem-Solving Abilities...70

7.3 The Future of Collaboration: Seamless Teamwork Through Brain-to-Brain Communication...73

7.4 Ethical Considerations in the Workplace: Addressing Issues of Privacy and Mental Strain...76

CHAPTER 8...78

BCIs in National Defense and Security: Ethical Dilemmas in a Technological Age...78

8.1 Brain-Computer Controlled Weapons: The Ethical Implications of Autonomous Warfare...78

8.2 Enhanced Soldier Performance: Ethical Considerations of Human Augmentation in the Military...80

8.3 Protecting National Security: Utilizing BCIs for Threat Detection and Intelligence Gathering...82

8.4 The Quest for International Cooperation: Establishing Regulations for BCIs in Military Applications...83

CHAPTER 9...88

The Philosophical and Societal Impact of BCIs: Reshaping Humanity......88

9.1 Redefining What it Means to be Human: The Blurring of Man and Machine...88

9.2 The Quest for Transhumanism: Upgrading Ourselves Beyond Biological Limitations...89

9.3 The Digital Divide: Ensuring Equitable Access to BCI Technology 92

9.4 The Future of Consciousness: Exploring the Potential for Machine Consciousness...94

CHAPTER 10...97

The Road Ahead: Navigating the Future of BCIs...97

10.1 Overcoming Technical Challenges: Advancing Accuracy, Security, and Accessibility of BCIs...97

10.2 The Role of Public Discourse: Fostering Open Communication About BCI Development...100

10.3 Building a Responsible Future: Ethical Frameworks for BCI Use and Development...102

10.4 A Look Towards the Horizon: The Untapped Potential of

Brain-Computer Interfaces.. 104

ABOUT THE AUTHOR... **109**

ACKNOWLEDGMENTS

I would like to extend my sincere gratitude to all those who have contributed to the realization of this book. First and foremost, I am indebted to my family for their unwavering support and encouragement throughout this endeavor. Their love and understanding have been my anchor in the stormy seas of writing.

I am deeply thankful to the experts whose guidance and insights have illuminated my path and enriched the content of this book. Their mentorship has been invaluable in shaping my understanding and refining my ideas.

I also extend my appreciation to those whose constructive feedback and insightful suggestions have helped polish this work to its finest form.

Furthermore, I am grateful to the countless individuals whose research, publications, and contributions have paved the way for the insights shared in these pages.

Last but not least, I express my heartfelt appreciation to the readers who embark on this journey with me. Your curiosity and engagement breathe life into these words, and it is for you that this book exists.

Thank you all for being part of this remarkable journey.

CHAPTER 1

UNVEILING THE MYSTERIOUS MIND

The human brain is perhaps the most complex and fascinating organ in existence. For millennia, it has been a source of wonder and speculation, driving philosophical inquiries and scientific exploration.

1.1 A Brief History of Brain Exploration: From Ancient Egypt to Modern Neuroscience

Our fascination with the brain stretches back to the dawn of civilization. The **ancient Egyptians**, during the height of their pharaonic culture (around 3100 BC), were the first to leave written records of brain anatomy. Their practice of mummification, while focused on preserving the body for the afterlife, offered a glimpse into the skull and its contents. The **Edwin Smith Papyrus**, a medical document dating back to 1700 BC, contains detailed descriptions of the brain and its surrounding membranes, including the cerebrospinal fluid. While they didn't understand its full function, the Egyptians laid the foundation for future exploration.

The baton was then passed to the **ancient Greeks**, who made significant contributions to our understanding of the brain. Philosophers like **Alcmaeon of Croton** (5th century BC) believed the brain was the seat of intelligence and sensation, a radical notion at the time. **Hippocrates**, the "Father of Medicine" (460-370 BC), challenged the prevailing belief that the heart was the center of thought and placed greater emphasis on the brain's role in human function. However, their understanding remained limited by the lack of sophisticated tools and ethical restrictions on human dissection.

The Hellenistic period (323-30 BC) witnessed a surge in anatomical research, particularly in the city of **Alexandria**. Here, physicians like **Herophilus of Chalcedon** (335-280

BC) and **Erasistratus of Chios** (304-250 BC) conducted groundbreaking dissections, differentiating between grey and white matter and mapping the brain's ventricles. Their work laid the groundwork for the Roman physician **Galen** (129-216 AD), who dominated medical thought for centuries. While some of Galen's theories were later proven inaccurate, his emphasis on empirical observation and detailed anatomical descriptions significantly advanced our knowledge of the brain.

The **Middle Ages** saw a decline in scientific inquiry due to religious dominance. However, the **Renaissance** (14th-17th centuries) marked a resurgence of interest in anatomy. Pioneering anatomists like **Andreas Vesalius** (1514-1564) challenged Galen's established theories through meticulous dissections. This paved the way for further advancements in brain research by **René Descartes** (1596-1650), who proposed the concept of **dualism**, separating the mind (immaterial) from the brain (physical). This idea of the mind as a non-physical entity dominated philosophical discussions for centuries.

The 19th century ushered in a new era of **neuroanatomy**. Scientists like **Camillo Golgi** (1843-1926) and **Santiago Ramón y Cajal** (1852-1934) developed staining techniques that revolutionized our understanding of the brain's cellular structure. They identified the fundamental unit of the nervous system, the **neuron**, and revealed its intricate connections, forming the basis of our understanding of **neural networks**.

The 20th century saw the rise of **neuroscience**, a dedicated field that integrated various disciplines to study the brain and nervous system. The development of the **electroencephalogram (EEG)** in the 1920s allowed scientists to measure electrical activity in the brain, opening doors to studying brain function. Technologies like **computerized tomography (CT scans)** and **magnetic resonance imaging (MRI)** in the latter half of the century provided unprecedented views of the brain's structure and activity.

Today, neuroscience is a rapidly evolving field. Techniques like **functional magnetic resonance imaging (fMRI)** allow us to map brain activity during tasks, revealing the intricate networks involved in various functions. **Genetics** is also playing an increasingly important role, helping us understand the influence of genes on brain development and function. The journey from the rudimentary observations of the Egyptians to the sophisticated tools of modern neuroscience demonstrates our ongoing quest to unravel the mysteries of the brain.

1.2 The Language of the Brain: Decoding Neurons and Neural Networks

The brain, despite its seemingly mushy consistency, is a marvel of cellular organization. Its basic building block is the **neuron**, a specialized cell responsible for transmitting information throughout the nervous system. Each neuron has three main parts:

- **Cell body (soma):** Contains the nucleus and controls

the neuron's overall function.

- **Dendrites:** Branching extensions that receive signals from other neurons.

- **Axon:** A long, slender fiber that transmits electrical signals to other neurons or muscles.

Neurons communicate with each other through specialized junctions called **synapses**. At a synapse, the axon of one neuron transmits an electrical signal across a tiny gap to the dendrites of another neuron. This signal can be either excitatory, encouraging the receiving neuron to fire an electrical impulse, or inhibitory, dampening its activity. The strength of these connections can be modified by experience, a phenomenon known as **synaptic plasticity**, which allows the brain to learn and adapt.

The intricate network of interconnected neurons forms the foundation of brain function. Billions of neurons communicate with each other in a complex dance of electrical signals, creating the patterns that underlie thought, emotion, and behavior. Understanding how these individual neurons work together is crucial to deciphering the language of the brain.

Types of Neurons:

There are various types of neurons, each specialized for a specific function:

- **Sensory neurons:** Transmit information about the environment from our senses (sight, touch, smell, etc.) to the brain.
- **Motor neurons:** Carry signals from the brain to our muscles, controlling movement.
- **Interneurons:** Form the vast majority of neurons in the brain, connecting sensory and motor neurons and processing information within the brain itself.

Neural Networks:

The interconnected web of neurons forms complex circuits called **neural networks**. These networks are responsible for processing information, generating thoughts, and coordinating behavior. Different brain regions have specialized networks dedicated to specific tasks, such as visual processing, language comprehension, and emotional regulation. The strength and organization of these networks are constantly changing throughout our lives as we learn, experience new things, and form memories.

Understanding neural networks is a key challenge in neuroscience. Researchers are using sophisticated computational models and imaging techniques to map the connections between different brain regions and understand how these networks give rise to complex mental functions.

1.3 Mapping the Mind: Exploring the Functional Areas of the Brain

The human brain can be broadly divided into two hemispheres, left and right, connected by a bundle of nerve fibers called the corpus callosum. Each hemisphere is further subdivided into various lobes, each with specialized functions. Here's a brief overview of some key regions:

- **Frontal lobe:** Located at the front of the brain, it is associated with higher-order functions like planning, decision-making, problem-solving, and personality.

- **Temporal lobe:** Situated on the side of the brain, it plays a crucial role in processing auditory information (hearing), memory formation, and some aspects of emotion.

- **Parietal lobe:** Found at the top of the brain, it is responsible for processing sensory information from the body (touch, pain, temperature), spatial awareness, and navigation.

- **Occipital lobe:** Located at the back of the brain, it is the primary visual processing center, responsible for interpreting visual information received from the eyes.

Beyond these main lobes, numerous specialized areas exist within the brain:

- **The amygdala:** Plays a central role in processing emotions, particularly fear and aggression.

- **The hippocampus:** Crucial for memory formation and retrieval.

- **The basal ganglia:** Involved in motor control, coordination, and habit formation.

Brain Mapping Techniques:

Modern neuroscience employs various techniques to map the brain's functional areas. These include:

- **Functional magnetic resonance imaging (fMRI):** Measures changes in blood flow to different brain regions, indicating areas activated during specific tasks.

- **Electroencephalography (EEG):** Measures electrical activity across the scalp, providing information about the overall brain state.

- **Transcranial magnetic stimulation (TMS):** Uses magnetic pulses to temporarily disrupt activity in specific brain regions, allowing researchers to study their function.

By mapping the brain, scientists can better understand the relationship between brain structure and function, leading to advancements in our understanding of neurological disorders, learning and memory, and even consciousness.

1.4 The Limits of the Human Brain: Understanding Our Cognitive Constraints

Despite its remarkable capabilities, the human brain has limitations. Here are some key areas:

- **Attention:** We can only focus on a limited amount of information at a time. Our ability to filter out distractions and concentrate on a specific task is crucial for efficient cognitive processing.
- **Memory:** While capable of storing vast amounts of information, our memory can be fallible. Factors like encoding, retrieval, and interference can affect what we remember and forget.
- **Problem-solving:** Our ability to solve problems can be limited by biases, heuristics (mental shortcuts),

and a lack of relevant information. We can fall prey to confirmation bias, seeking information that confirms existing beliefs, or fall victim to mental fatigue, hindering our ability to think critically after extended periods of work.

- **Learning:** While we have a remarkable capacity for learning throughout life, our ability to acquire new information and skills can be influenced by factors like age, motivation, and prior knowledge.

These limitations are not necessarily flaws but inherent aspects of our biological makeup. However, understanding these constraints is crucial for optimizing our cognitive performance. By employing strategies to manage attention, improve memory formation, and mitigate biases in decision-making, we can learn to work within the boundaries of our brains and maximize our potential.

The Future of Brain Exploration:

The quest to understand the brain is far from over. New

technologies and research advancements are constantly pushing the boundaries of our knowledge. Fields like **connectomics** are focusing on mapping the intricate wiring diagrams of the brain, while **neurogenetics** explores the influence of genes on brain function and behavior.

As we continue to unravel the mysteries of the brain, we stand to gain a deeper understanding of ourselves, opening doors to advancements in healthcare, education, and even human-computer interaction through Brain-Computer Interfaces (BCIs), a topic explored in later chapters. However, with this progress comes the need for ethical considerations as we delve deeper into the realm of the human mind.

This chapter has provided a brief historical overview of brain exploration, exploring the fundamental unit of the brain – the neuron – and its role in forming neural networks. We have also discussed the functional areas of the brain and the limitations inherent to our cognitive abilities. By understanding these aspects, we can embark on a journey of further exploration, unlocking the vast

potential that lies within the human brain.

CHAPTER 2

BIRTH OF THE BRAIN-COMPUTER INTERFACE (BCI): A
TECHNOLOGICAL REVOLUTION

The human brain, with its immense processing power and intricate neural networks, has long captured the imagination of scientists and science fiction writers alike. The concept of a **Brain-Computer Interface (BCI)**, a technology that allows direct communication and control between the brain and a computer, has transcended the realm of fantasy and is now a rapidly evolving field with the potential to revolutionize various aspects of human life.

2.1 From Science Fiction to Reality: The Early Dreams of BCI Technology

The idea of a BCI has captivated humanity for decades. Early glimpses of this technology can be found in science fiction literature, where authors envisioned telepathic communication and mind-controlled machines. In the 1920s, visionary scientist **Hans Berger** first documented the existence of brainwaves through electroencephalography (EEG). This discovery laid the foundation for the possibility of measuring and interpreting brain activity, a crucial step towards developing BCIs.

The mid-20th century saw a surge in interest in BCI technology. Pioneering figures like **Dr. Jose Delgado** conducted experiments with electrical brain stimulation in animals, demonstrating the potential to influence behavior. In the 1960s, researchers like **Dr. Benjamin Libet** explored the relationship between brain activity and conscious thought, sparking discussions about the possibility of reading minds using BCIs.

The 1970s witnessed significant advancements. Researchers like **Dr. Jacques Vidal** developed early BCI prototypes that allowed monkeys to control cursors on a computer screen using brainwaves. These early experiments, while limited, paved the way for further development of BCI technology.

2.2 Non-invasive vs. Invasive BCIs: Weighing the Risks and Rewards

BCIs can be categorized into two main types based on their level of invasiveness:

- **Non-invasive BCIs:** These systems utilize techniques like EEG, magnetoencephalography (MEG), and near-infrared spectroscopy (NIRS) to measure brain activity from the scalp without penetrating the skull. They are generally considered safer and more widely applicable, but the resolution of the signal can be lower compared to invasive BCIs.

- **Invasive BCIs:** These involve surgically implanting electrodes directly on the brain surface or within brain tissue. This allows for a more precise and high-resolution signal but carries inherent risks of surgery and infection. Invasive BCIs are typically used in research settings or for individuals with severe disabilities where non-invasive techniques are not effective.

The choice between non-invasive and invasive BCIs depends on several factors:

- **The desired application:** For basic control functions, non-invasive BCIs may suffice. However, for more complex tasks requiring high-resolution signals, invasive BCIs might be necessary.

- **The user's health and comfort:** Invasive surgery carries risks, and not everyone is comfortable with the idea of implants in their brain.

- **Technological advancements:** Non-invasive BCI technology is constantly evolving, and the gap in signal resolution between invasive and non-invasive methods is narrowing.

2.3 How Does a BCI Work? Translating Brain Signals into Actionable Commands

Regardless of the type of BCI, the basic principle remains the same: translating brain activity into commands that can be understood and acted upon by a computer. Here's a simplified breakdown of the process:

1. **Brain Signal Acquisition:** Non-invasive BCIs use sensors placed on the scalp to detect electrical activity or changes in blood flow. Invasive BCIs use implanted electrodes to capture neural signals directly from the brain tissue.

2. **Signal Processing:** The raw brain signals are complex and require extensive processing. Specialized algorithms are used to filter out noise, identify specific patterns of brain activity, and translate them into meaningful commands.

3. **Command Decoding:** Once the relevant brain

signals are identified, they are mapped to specific actions or outputs, such as controlling a cursor on a screen, triggering a robotic arm, or sending a text message.

4. **Brain-Computer Interaction:** The decoded commands are then used to control external devices, software applications, or even other computers in real-time.

Challenges in BCI Development:

Despite significant progress, BCI technology still faces challenges:

- **Signal Accuracy:** Interpreting brain signals reliably is complex, and current technology is susceptible to noise and user variability.

- **Limited Bandwidth:** The information transfer rate

between the brain and the computer is still limited compared to traditional input methods.

- **Calibration and Training:** BCIs often require extensive calibration and user training to achieve optimal performance.

2.4 The Future of BCI Design: Addressing Challenges and Pushing the Boundaries

Researchers are actively working to overcome the limitations of BCI technology. Here are some promising areas of development:

- **Advanced Signal Processing:** Machine learning algorithms and artificial intelligence are being employed to improve the accuracy and efficiency of interpreting brain signals.

- **Brain-Machine Interfaces (BMIs):** BMIs are a specific type of BCI that focuses on controlling external devices like prosthetics. Advancements in neural implants and decoding algorithms are leading to more intuitive and natural control of these devices.

- **Brain-to-Brain Communication (BBCI):** This emerging field explores the possibility of direct communication between brains without the need for spoken or written language. While still in its early stages, BBCI holds the potential for revolutionizing communication and collaboration.

- **Non-invasive BCI Advancements:** Improvements in sensor technology and signal processing are leading to more powerful non-invasive BCIs that could provide a wider range of applications with better user comfort.

- **Closed-Loop BCIs:** These systems incorporate feedback mechanisms, allowing the BCI to adjust its behavior based on the user's brain activity and the response of the external device. This creates a more dynamic and interactive experience for the user.

Ethical Considerations:

As BCI technology advances, ethical considerations become increasingly important.

- **Privacy and Security:** Protecting user brain data from unauthorized access is crucial.

- **Brain Hacking:** The possibility of malicious actors manipulating BCIs raises concerns about user safety and control.

- **Augmentation and Equity:** Access to BCI technology should be equitable, and the potential for widening the gap between those who can afford this technology and those who cannot needs careful consideration.

- **The Nature of Consciousness:** BCIs raise questions about the nature of consciousness and free will. If we can directly control devices with our thoughts, does that blur the line between human and machine?

The future of BCI technology is full of possibilities. As we continue to refine existing technologies and explore new avenues, BCIs have the potential to transform various aspects of human life, from healthcare and communication to entertainment and education. However, it is crucial to address the ethical challenges alongside technological advancements to ensure a responsible and beneficial future for BCIs.

We have explored the history of BCI technology, its different types, the basic working principles, and the challenges it faces. We have also discussed the exciting possibilities on the horizon and the ethical considerations that need to be addressed. As we move forward, BCIs hold the promise of becoming a powerful tool for enhancing human capabilities and expanding our understanding of the brain itself.

CHAPTER 3

BCIs for Healthcare: Restoring Function and
Enhancing Lives

The human brain is an incredibly adaptable organ, but
when injury or disease strikes, it can lead to a loss of
function that can significantly impact a person's quality of
life. Brain-Computer Interfaces (BCIs) are emerging as a
game-changer in the field of healthcare, offering new hope
for individuals with various neurological conditions.

3.1 Aiding Individuals with Paralysis: Regaining
Control Through Thought-Controlled Devices

For people with paralysis caused by conditions like spinal
cord injuries, stroke, or amyotrophic lateral sclerosis
(ALS), regaining control over their bodies can be a
life-altering transformation. BCIs offer a revolutionary
approach to achieving this goal.

- **Motor Cortex BCIs:** These systems focus on decoding brain activity in the motor cortex, the region responsible for planning and initiating movement. By identifying patterns of brain activity associated with specific movement intentions, BCIs can translate these thoughts into commands that control external devices.

Here are some examples of how BCIs are helping individuals with paralysis:

- **Controlling Robotic Arms:** Invasive BCIs can allow paralyzed individuals to control robotic limbs with remarkable dexterity, enabling them to perform tasks like eating, dressing, and interacting with their environment.

- **Assistive Technologies:** BCIs can be used to operate wheelchairs, control smart home devices, and even navigate virtual environments, increasing independence and improving quality of life.

- **Brain-Controlled Exoskeletons:** These robotic suits powered by BCI technology can help individuals with paralysis stand, walk, and even participate in physical therapy exercises, fostering a sense of agency and promoting physical well-being.

Challenges and Advancements:

While BCI technology offers immense potential for individuals with paralysis, there are still challenges to overcome.

- **Accuracy and Speed:** Improving the accuracy and speed of BCI control remains a key focus. Users need real-time, intuitive control over devices for practical applications.

- **Calibration and Training:** BCIs often require extensive user calibration and training to achieve optimal performance. Simplifying these processes will be crucial for broader adoption.

- **Cost and Accessibility:** Current BCI technology can be expensive, and ensuring equitable access for all patients is a critical consideration.

Researchers are actively working on addressing these challenges, and advancements in areas like machine learning and brain-machine interfaces (BMIs) are leading to more sophisticated and user-friendly control systems.

3.2 Communication Regained: Empowering People with Speech Loss to Express Themselves

For individuals who have lost the ability to speak due to conditions like stroke, ALS, or severe brain injuries, communication can become a significant barrier. BCIs offer a promising new avenue for restoring communication and reconnecting with the world.

- **Speech Augmentation BCIs:** These systems focus on decoding brain activity associated with speech production. By analyzing patterns of brain activity, BCIs can predict what a person intends to say and generate synthetic speech or control text-to-speech applications.

- **BCI-based Assistive Spelling Devices:** These systems allow users to spell words letter by letter using BCI control. This allows for slower but more deliberate communication compared to speech augmentation.

The Impact of Communication Restoration:

Regaining the ability to communicate can have a profound impact on the lives of individuals with speech loss. It allows them to express their needs and desires, participate in conversations, and maintain social connections, leading to a significant improvement in their quality of life and well-being.

Challenges and Considerations:

While BCI-based communication holds immense promise, it's important to consider some challenges:

- **Understanding Context:** BCIs currently focus on decoding intended words, not necessarily the full context of communication. Integrating emotional tone and nonverbal cues remains an ongoing area of research.

- **User Interface Design:** BCI interfaces for communication need to be user-friendly and adaptable to individual needs and communication styles.

- **Ethical Considerations:** As communication technology advances, ensuring user privacy and control over their data is crucial.

Despite these challenges, BCI technology is rapidly evolving, offering new hope for individuals who have lost their ability to speak. The ability to express oneself freely is a fundamental human right, and BCIs are becoming a powerful tool in restoring this right for those who have lost it.

3.3 Beyond Physical Limitations: Exploring BCIs for Mental Health Treatment

BCIs are not just limited to restoring physical function; they also hold promise for aiding in the treatment of mental health conditions. Here are some potential applications:

- **Neurofeedback:** This technique uses real-time brain activity feedback to help individuals learn to regulate their brainwaves. It has shown promise in treating anxiety, depression, and ADHD.

- **BCI-based Addiction Treatment:** BCIs can be used

to help individuals with addiction identify and manage cravings. By providing real-time feedback on brain activity associated with cravings, BCIs can help users develop strategies for self-regulation and relapse prevention.

- **BCI-Augmented Therapy:** BCIs can be integrated with traditional therapy approaches to create more personalized and targeted interventions. For example, BCIs could be used to monitor a patient's emotional state during therapy sessions, allowing therapists to tailor their approach in real-time.

Challenges and Considerations:

While the potential of BCIs for mental health treatment is exciting, there are important considerations:

- **Efficacy and Long-Term Effects:** More research is needed to establish the long-term efficacy and safety of BCI-based interventions for mental health conditions.

- **Ethical Concerns:** Privacy issues and potential manipulation of brain activity raise ethical concerns that need careful consideration.

- **Accessibility and Equity:** Ensuring equitable access to BCI technology for mental health treatment is crucial to avoid widening existing disparities in healthcare.

Despite these challenges, the potential of BCIs for mental health treatment is undeniable. As research progresses, BCIs could become valuable tools in the fight against mental illness, offering new hope for millions of people worldwide.

3.4 The Ethical Landscape of Neurorehabilitation: Balancing Benefits with Patient Autonomy

The use of BCIs in healthcare raises a number of ethical considerations that require careful attention. Here are some key areas of concern:

- **Informed Consent:** Patients undergoing BCI therapy need to be fully informed of the risks and benefits of the technology, and their consent must be obtained freely and without coercion.

- **Patient Autonomy:** Brain-computer interfaces interact with a person's most private thoughts and intentions. Ensuring patient autonomy and control over their data is paramount.

- **Brain Hacking and Security:** As BCI technology becomes more sophisticated, the risk of unauthorized access to brain data becomes a concern. Robust security measures must be implemented to protect patient privacy.

- **Equity and Access:** BCI technology is expensive, and ensuring equitable access for all patients, regardless of socioeconomic status, is crucial.

- **The Nature of Consciousness:** BCIs raise questions about the nature of consciousness and free will. As we interface with technology through our thoughts, where do we draw the line between human and machine?

Addressing these ethical concerns is crucial for ensuring the responsible and beneficial development of BCIs in healthcare. Open dialogue and collaboration between scientists, ethicists, policymakers, and the public are essential to create a framework for ethical neurorehabilitation practices.

BCIs are revolutionizing healthcare, offering new hope for individuals with various neurological conditions. From restoring physical function and communication to aiding in mental health treatment, the potential applications of BCIs are vast and continue to expand. However, it is crucial to acknowledge and address the ethical considerations that accompany this powerful technology. By balancing innovation with responsibility, BCIs can become a transformative force in healthcare, improving lives, and promoting human well-being.

CHAPTER 4

BCIs for Augmentation: Redefining Human Potential

Brain-Computer Interfaces (BCIs) are not just about restoring lost function; they hold the potential to push the boundaries of human capability.

4.1 Beyond Human Limits: Enhancing Sensory Perception and Cognitive Abilities

Imagine a world where you can see beyond the visible spectrum, hear faint sounds from afar, or access information directly through your thoughts. BCIs are opening doors to augmenting our sensory perception and cognitive abilities in ways never before imagined.

- **Sensory Augmentation:** BCIs can be used to restore or enhance sensory capabilities lost due to injury or disease. For example, visual prosthetics can provide sight to blind individuals, while auditory BCIs can help individuals with hearing loss perceive sound. Additionally, BCIs can potentially enhance our natural senses, allowing us to see in low-light conditions or hear sounds at higher or lower frequencies than our natural range.

- **Cognitive Enhancement:** BCIs have the potential to boost our cognitive abilities. Imagine directly accessing information through your thoughts, bypassing the need for traditional learning methods. BCIs could also be used to improve memory, focus, and decision-making, allowing us to process information and solve problems more efficiently.

Challenges and Considerations:

Enhancing sensory and cognitive abilities through BCIs raises some critical questions:

- **Safety and Long-Term Effects:** The long-term effects of BCI augmentation on the brain are not fully understood. Safety assessments and rigorous testing are crucial.

- **Sensory Overload:** Enhancing our senses beyond their natural limits could lead to information overload and sensory fatigue. Careful calibration and user control over augmented sensations are essential.

- **The Definition of "Human":** As we augment our abilities with technology, where do we draw the line between human and machine? Is enhanced cognition still "natural"?

4.2 The Rise of the Cyborg: Merging Human and Machine Intelligence

The concept of a cyborg, a being with both biological and

technological components, has long captured our imagination. BCIs could be the key to unlocking this future.

- **Brain-Machine Interfaces (BMIs):** BMIs are a specific type of BCI designed for seamless interaction with external devices like prosthetics or robotic systems. Advancements in BMIs could allow for more intuitive control of these devices, blurring the line between human and machine.

- **Augmented Reality (AR) and Virtual Reality (VR) Integration:** BCIs could be used to seamlessly interact with AR and VR environments. Imagine controlling virtual objects with your thoughts or manipulating the virtual world through your brainwaves.

The potential for merging human and machine intelligence is vast, and it raises some fascinating possibilities:

- **Enhanced Problem-Solving:** By combining human creativity with the processing power of machines, we could tackle complex problems in entirely new ways.

- **Augmented Creativity:** BCIs could provide artists and designers with new tools for creative expression, fostering a new era of human-machine collaboration in artistic endeavors.

Challenges and Considerations:

Merging human and machine intelligence necessitates careful consideration of ethical issues:

- **Loss of Autonomy:** As we rely more on technology for cognitive functions, could we lose some degree of autonomy over our own thoughts and decisions?

- **The Digital Divide:** Unequal access to BCI

augmentation technology could exacerbate existing social and economic inequalities.

- **The Weaponization of BMIs:** The potential military applications of BMIs raise concerns about the weaponization of human-machine interfaces.

4.3 Brain-Computer Interfaces in Education: Personalized Learning and Knowledge Augmentation

Education is another field where BCIs hold immense potential. Here's how BCIs could transform learning:

- **Personalized Learning:** BCIs could monitor a student's brain activity to assess their understanding and tailor instruction accordingly. This personalized approach could lead to more effective and engaging learning experiences.

- **Augmented Knowledge Acquisition:** Imagine

directly accessing information through BCIs, bypassing traditional learning methods. BCIs could offer students a new way to learn vast amounts of information quickly and efficiently.

- **Neurofeedback for Learning Enhancement:** Real-time feedback on brain activity could help students learn to focus better, improve their memory, and overcome learning challenges.

The potential benefits of BCIs in education are vast, but there are also considerations:

- **Equity and Access:** Ensuring all students have access to BCI technology is crucial to avoid widening the education gap.

- **Academic Integrity:** BCIs could potentially be used for cheating, which necessitates robust anti-cheating measures.

- **The Future of Educators:** The role of teachers might evolve as BCIs take on a more prominent role in knowledge delivery.

4.4 Ethical Considerations of Human Enhancement: Ensuring Equity and Preventing Abuse

The prospect of human enhancement through BCIs is exhilarating, but it also raises a multitude of ethical concerns that demand careful consideration:

- **Equity and Access:** BCI augmentation technology is likely to be expensive, and ensuring equitable access for everyone is paramount. We cannot create a situation where only the wealthy can afford to enhance their cognitive or sensory abilities.

- **The Commodification of Enhancement:** Will BCI augmentation become a commodity, further widening the gap between the haves and have-nots? Will cognitive enhancement become a prerequisite for certain jobs or social circles?

- **Preventing Abuse:** BCI technology could be misused for malicious purposes. For instance, it could be used to manipulate people's thoughts or emotions, or even to create addictive experiences within virtual environments. Robust safeguards are needed to prevent such abuses.

- **The Definition of "Natural":** As we augment our abilities with technology, what does it mean to be human? Will enhanced individuals be seen as superior to those who remain unaugmented? These questions need open discussion and ethical frameworks to guide development.

- **Regulation and Oversight:** As BCI technology advances, robust regulatory frameworks are essential to ensure its safe and ethical development and application. Open dialogue and collaboration between scientists, ethicists, policymakers, and the public are crucial for creating responsible BCI augmentation practices.

4.5 Conclusion: A Future of Human Potential, Amplified

Brain-Computer Interfaces hold immense potential for augmenting human capabilities, pushing the boundaries of what we can perceive, think, and achieve. From enhancing sensory experiences and cognitive abilities to merging human and machine intelligence, BCIs offer a glimpse into a future where technology seamlessly integrates with our biological selves. However, alongside the excitement lies the responsibility to ensure responsible development and ethical considerations. By prioritizing equitable access, preventing abuse, and fostering open discussions about the nature of humanness, we can harness the power of BCIs to create a brighter future for all.

This chapter has explored the potential of BCIs for enhancing human capabilities. We have discussed the possibilities of sensory augmentation, cognitive enhancement, human-machine intelligence integration, and BCI applications in education. We have also addressed the crucial ethical considerations that accompany this powerful technology. As we move forward, BCIs have the potential to become a transformative force, not just in healthcare, but in all aspects of human life. The future of human potential lies amplified, and BCIs will undoubtedly play a significant role in shaping that future.

CHAPTER 5

BCIs in Gaming and Entertainment: Blurring the Lines Between Reality and Fantasy

The world of entertainment is constantly evolving, seeking new ways to immerse audiences and engage players. Brain-Computer Interfaces (BCIs) are poised to revolutionize this landscape, offering a level of interactivity and control never before experienced.

5.1 The Future of Gaming: Immersive Experiences Controlled by Your Thoughts

Imagine a world where you don't need a controller or keyboard to play a game. With BCIs, players could control in-game actions and navigate virtual environments directly through their thoughts. This level of immersive control opens doors to entirely new gaming experiences:

- **Thought-Controlled Gameplay:** BCIs could allow players to control characters' movements, actions, and even spells with their thoughts. Imagine battling enemies, solving puzzles, or exploring vast landscapes, all through the power of your mind.

- **Enhanced Emotional Immersion:** BCIs could potentially detect and respond to a player's emotional state. Games could adapt difficulty levels, storylines, or even the virtual environment based on a player's emotional response, creating a truly personalized and dynamic experience.

- **Augmented Reality (AR) and Virtual Reality (VR) Integration:** BCIs could seamlessly integrate with AR and VR experiences, blurring the lines between the real and virtual worlds. Players could interact with virtual objects or manipulate environments using their thoughts, creating a truly immersive experience.

Beyond Gaming:

The applications of BCIs in entertainment extend beyond traditional video games:

- **Interactive Storytelling:** BCIs could create interactive stories where the narrative unfolds based on the reader's or viewer's thoughts and emotions. Imagine a choose-your-own-adventure story where your decisions are made not by button presses but by your brain activity.

- **Interactive Art and Music:** BCIs could allow artists and musicians to create works that respond to the audience's brainwaves in real-time. This could lead to new forms of interactive art installations or even musical performances that adapt based on the emotional state of the audience.

The possibilities for BCIs in entertainment are vast and continue to evolve, offering a future where the boundaries between players, viewers, and the content itself become increasingly fluid.

5.2 Beyond Entertainment: BCIs for Art, Music, and Creative Expression

BCIs have the potential to become powerful tools for creative expression:

- **Thought-Controlled Instruments:** Imagine composing music or creating visual art directly through your thoughts. BCIs could allow artists to translate their mental imagery and emotions into creative works, opening doors to entirely new forms of artistic expression.

- **Enhanced Accessibility:** BCIs could provide new avenues for creative expression for individuals with disabilities. Those who might struggle with traditional methods of creation could utilize BCIs to express themselves creatively.

- **Collaborative Art and Music Creation:** BCIs could facilitate collaborative art and music creation where multiple minds interact through brainwaves, leading to unique and innovative artistic endeavors.

The potential for BCIs to empower artists and redefine creative expression is significant, but challenges remain.

5.3 The Challenges of Brain-Computer Interaction: Ensuring User Experience and Security

While BCIs offer exciting possibilities in entertainment, there are challenges to overcome:

- **Accuracy and Calibration:** BCI technology is still under development, and ensuring accurate and reliable interpretation of brain signals is crucial for a positive user experience.

- **User Fatigue and Mental Strain:** Concentrating on controlling a game or creative tool with your thoughts can be mentally taxing. Measures to prevent user fatigue and ensure comfortable interaction are essential.

- **Security and Privacy Concerns:** BCI technology raises concerns about data security and privacy. Measures to protect user brain data from unauthorized access are crucial.

5.4 The Ethical Debate: Blurring the Lines Between Player and Character

The immersive nature of BCI-powered entertainment raises ethical questions:

- **Addiction and Escapism:** The highly immersive nature of BCI games could lead to addiction and difficulty distinguishing between the real and virtual worlds.

- **Loss of Control and Agency:** As the line between player and character blurs, what level of control do players retain over their actions within the game?

- **The Nature of Play:** Does BCI-based gameplay undermine the traditional aspects of play, such as skill development and strategic thinking?

These are complex questions that require ongoing discussion and ethical frameworks to guide the development and use of BCIs in entertainment.

Brain-Computer Interfaces hold immense potential for revolutionizing entertainment, offering unprecedented levels of immersion and control. However, alongside the excitement lies the responsibility to address challenges like user experience, security, and ethical considerations. By prioritizing responsible development, fostering open discussions, and addressing ethical concerns, BCIs can become powerful tools for creating transformative and enriching entertainment experiences.

The future of entertainment lies at the intersection of technology and human imagination. BCIs offer a glimpse into a world where the boundaries between players, viewers, and the content itself become increasingly fluid. Imagine attending a concert where the music adapts to your emotions, or exploring a virtual world where your thoughts control your character's actions. These are just a few possibilities on the horizon.

However, it's crucial to acknowledge the challenges that need to be addressed:

- **Balancing Innovation and User Experience:** BCI technology must be user-friendly, reliable, and comfortable to wear for extended periods. Balancing the need for advanced functionality with user comfort is essential.

- **Security and Privacy Safeguards:** Robust security measures are needed to protect user brain data from unauthorized access and potential misuse. Clear user consent protocols and data privacy regulations must be established.

- **The Importance of Ethical Frameworks:** Open dialogue and collaboration between developers, ethicists, and the public are crucial for creating responsible BCI entertainment experiences. Ethical considerations such as addiction prevention, player agency, and the nature of play require careful attention.

As BCI technology matures, it has the potential to not only redefine entertainment but also foster new forms of creative expression and artistic collaboration. By embracing the power of BCIs while acknowledging the ethical considerations, we can usher in a new era of immersive and enriching entertainment experiences for all.

CHAPTER 6

BCIs in Communication: Revolutionizing How We Interact with the World

Communication is the cornerstone of human connection. Brain-Computer Interfaces (BCIs) hold the potential to revolutionize the way we interact with the world, offering new avenues for expressing ourselves, understanding others, and even achieving a level of mind-to-mind communication that was once relegated to science fiction.

6.1 Thought-Controlled Communication: From Telepathy to Direct Brain-to-Brain Interaction

Imagine a world where you can communicate your thoughts and feelings directly, without the need for spoken or written language. BCIs are opening doors to new forms of thought-controlled communication:

- **Speech Augmentation and Rehabilitation:** For individuals who have lost the ability to speak due to conditions like stroke, ALS, or severe brain injuries, BCIs can offer a powerful tool for regaining their voice. These systems can decode brain activity associated with speech production and translate it into synthesized speech or control text-to-speech applications.

- **Augmentative and Alternative Communication (AAC):** BCIs can provide new options for individuals with communication disabilities who rely on AAC methods. Brain-controlled interfaces could offer faster and more intuitive communication compared to traditional methods.

- **Brain-to-Brain Communication (BBCI):** This emerging field explores the possibility of direct communication between brains without the need for spoken or written language. While still in its early stages, BBCI holds the potential to revolutionize how we connect and collaborate, enabling a level of understanding that transcends spoken words.

The Benefits of Thought-Controlled Communication:

Thought-controlled communication offers numerous benefits:

- **Improved Accessibility:** BCIs can provide new communication options for individuals with disabilities, fostering greater social inclusion and participation.

- **Enhanced Efficiency and Speed:** Direct thought communication could potentially be faster and more efficient than traditional methods of communication.

- **Nuanced Expression:** BCIs might allow for the transmission of not just words but also the emotional context of communication, leading to richer and more meaningful interactions.

Challenges and Considerations:

Despite the potential, there are challenges to overcome:

- **Accuracy and Decoding Complexity:** Decoding complex thought patterns and translating them into understandable messages remains a challenge.

- **Privacy and Security Concerns:** Direct brain communication raises concerns about privacy and the potential for unauthorized access to one's thoughts.

- **The Future of Language:** Will the widespread adoption of BCI communication lead to a decline in spoken and written language skills?

6.2 The Future of Social Media: Sharing Thoughts and Emotions Directly

Social media has transformed the way we connect, but what if we could share not just words and pictures, but our thoughts and emotions directly? BCIs could revolutionize social media in the following ways:

- **Direct Thought Sharing:** Imagine a social media platform where you can share your thoughts and feelings directly with others, bypassing the need for text or emojis. This could lead to a more authentic and nuanced form of social interaction.

- **Enhanced Empathy and Understanding:** By sharing brain activity associated with emotions, BCIs could foster a deeper level of empathy and understanding between people on social media.

- **Ethical Considerations and Privacy Concerns:** Sharing thoughts and emotions directly raises significant ethical concerns about privacy, manipulation, and the potential misuse of personal information.

The potential for BCI-based social media is vast, but careful consideration must be given to the ethical implications.

6.3 Language Learning Reimagined: Accelerated Learning Through Brain-Computer Interfaces

Language learning can be a challenging and time-consuming process. BCIs offer a glimpse into a future of accelerated language acquisition:

- **Brainwave Biomarkers for Language Learning:** BCIs could identify brainwave patterns associated with successful language learning, allowing for personalized learning approaches.

- **Augmented Language Immersion:** BCIs could be integrated with virtual reality environments to create immersive language learning experiences that directly stimulate the brain's language learning centers.

- **Direct Language Acquisition:** While still theoretical, the future might hold possibilities for directly transferring language skills from one brain to another through BCIs.

The Democratization of Language Learning:

BCIs have the potential to democratize language learning by making it faster, more efficient, and accessible to a wider range of learners.

Challenges and Considerations:

- **The Role of Traditional Learning Methods:** Would BCIs replace traditional language learning methods entirely, or would they serve as a complementary tool?

- **Equity and Access:** Ensuring equitable access to BCI-based language learning technologies is crucial to avoid widening existing educational disparities.

- **The Cultural Aspects of Language:** Language learning involves more than just vocabulary and grammar. How would BCIs account for the cultural nuances and social aspects of language acquisition?

6.4 The Power of Empathy: Fostering Deeper Understanding Through Shared Brain Activity

Communication is not just about transmitting information; it's also about understanding the thoughts and feelings of others. BCIs offer the potential to foster empathy and deeper connections between people:

- **Shared Brain Activity for Empathy Training:**

Imagine being able to experience another person's emotions through shared brain activity. BCIs could be used to train empathy in individuals with social challenges like autism spectrum disorder.

- **Conflict Resolution and Negotiation:** BCIs could potentially be used in conflict resolution or negotiation situations to help parties understand each other's emotional states and perspectives, leading to more productive interactions.

- **The Future of Human Connection:** While the idea of directly sharing thoughts and emotions raises privacy concerns, BCIs could also foster a deeper level of human connection based on mutual understanding and empathy.

The Ethical Considerations of Shared Brain Activity:

The potential for sharing brain activity raises significant ethical questions:

- **Informed Consent and Manipulation:** Sharing

brain activity requires informed consent, and safeguards against manipulation or coercion are crucial.

- **Privacy and Security Concerns:** The technology to directly access and interpret brain activity raises significant privacy and security concerns. Robust safeguards to protect personal information are essential.

- **The Nature of Human Interaction:** Does direct brain-to-brain communication undermine the importance of verbal and nonverbal communication in fostering human connection?

Brain-Computer Interfaces have the potential to revolutionize the way we communicate, offering new avenues for self-expression, understanding others, and even achieving a level of mind-to-mind communication that was once science fiction. From thought-controlled communication to social media platforms that share emotions directly, BCIs open doors to a future of richer and more nuanced human interaction. However, alongside the excitement lies the responsibility to address challenges like privacy, security, and the potential impact on traditional forms of communication. By prioritizing responsible development, fostering open discussions, and addressing ethical concerns, we can harness the power of BCIs to create a future where technology enhances our ability to connect, empathize, and understand each other on a deeper level.

CHAPTER 7

BCIs in the Workplace: Transforming How We Work and Learn

The workplace is constantly evolving, and Brain-Computer Interfaces (BCIs) are poised to play a significant role in this transformation. By offering new avenues for enhancing cognitive performance, optimizing skill development, and facilitating seamless collaboration, BCIs hold the potential to revolutionize the way we work and learn.

7.1 Increased Productivity and Efficiency: Enhancing Cognitive Performance in the Workplace

Imagine a world where workers can directly access information, analyze data sets with their thoughts, and even improve their focus and memory through brain-computer interfaces. BCIs offer the potential to enhance cognitive performance in the workplace in several ways:

- **Augmented Information Processing:** BCIs could be used to display relevant information directly in a worker's field of vision, reducing the need to switch between screens and documents, and improving information processing efficiency.

- **Neurofeedback for Cognitive Enhancement:** Real-time feedback on brain activity levels could help workers identify and manage distraction, improve focus, and enhance overall cognitive performance.

- **Brain-Machine Interfaces for Complex Tasks:** BMIs could be used to control complex machinery or robotic systems with greater precision and efficiency, particularly in fields like manufacturing or surgery.

The Benefits of Enhanced Cognitive Performance:

Increased cognitive performance in the workplace can lead to several benefits:

- **Improved Productivity and Efficiency:** Workers who can access information faster, focus better, and make decisions more efficiently are likely to be more productive.

- **Reduced Work-Related Errors:** Improved focus and decision-making can lead to fewer errors, enhancing workplace safety and reducing costs.

- **Enhanced Employee Satisfaction:** Feeling empowered with improved cognitive abilities can lead to increased employee satisfaction and engagement.

Challenges and Considerations:

While exciting, there are challenges to address:

- **Calibration and Individual Differences:** BCI performance can vary significantly between individuals. Ensuring proper calibration and tailoring the technology to individual needs is crucial.

- **The Cost of Implementation:** BCI technology is still under development, and the cost of implementation could be a barrier for some businesses.

- **The Definition of "Normal" Cognition:** Does enhancing cognitive abilities through BCIs create an unfair advantage for some workers? What constitutes "normal" cognitive performance in the workplace?

7.2 Brain-Computer Training: Optimizing Skill

Development and Problem-Solving Abilities

The process of learning and acquiring new skills can be time-consuming and challenging. BCIs offer a glimpse into a future of accelerated skill development and enhanced problem-solving abilities:

- **Personalized Training Programs:** BCIs could analyze brain activity patterns associated with skill acquisition and tailor training programs to an individual's learning style and needs.

- **Neurofeedback for Skill Improvement:** Real-time feedback on brain activity can help individuals identify areas needing improvement and adjust their learning strategies accordingly.

- **Augmented Reality (AR) Integration:** BCIs could be integrated with AR environments to create immersive training experiences that stimulate the brain and accelerate skill development.

The Benefits of Brain-Computer Training:

Brain-computer training in the workplace offers several benefits:

- **Reduced Training Time and Costs:** By personalizing training and optimizing learning, BCIs can potentially reduce the time and resources required for employee training.

- **Improved Skill Retention:** By actively engaging the brain during learning, BCIs could lead to better skill retention and knowledge application in the workplace.

- **Fostering a Culture of Continuous Learning:** BCIs can create a more dynamic and engaging learning environment, encouraging continuous skill development and knowledge acquisition.

Challenges and Considerations:

- **The Role of Traditional Training Methods:** Would BCIs replace traditional training methods entirely, or would they serve as a complementary tool?

- **Equity and Access:** Ensuring all employees have access to BCI-based training opportunities is crucial to avoid widening existing skill gaps.

- **The Importance of Human Expertise:** While BCIs can enhance training, human expertise remains essential for mentorship, guidance, and fostering critical thinking skills.

7.3 The Future of Collaboration: Seamless Teamwork Through Brain-to-Brain Communication

Effective communication and collaboration are essential for success in today's workplace. BCIs offer the potential to revolutionize teamwork by facilitating a more seamless exchange of ideas and information:

- **Shared Brain Activity for Enhanced Collaboration:** While the technology is in its early stages, BCIs might one day allow teams to share ideas and information directly through brain activity, fostering a deeper level of understanding and collaboration.

- **Brain-Computer Interfaces for Remote Teams:** BCIs could facilitate more efficient collaboration between geographically dispersed teams by enabling real-time sharing of information and insights directly through brain-computer interfaces.

- **Augmented Decision-Making:** BCIs could analyze brain activity patterns of team members to identify potential biases or areas of disagreement, leading to more informed and objective collective decisions.

The Future of Teamwork:

BCIs have the potential to revolutionize teamwork by fostering deeper collaboration, enhanced communication, and more efficient decision-making processes. However, there are challenges to consider:

- **The Importance of Social Interaction:** While BCIs can facilitate information exchange, they cannot replicate the importance of social interaction, trust-building, and nonverbal communication in successful teamwork.

- **Ethical Considerations of Brain Sharing:** The idea of sharing brain activity raises concerns about privacy, security, and potential manipulation within team dynamics.

- **The Future of Leadership:** How will leadership styles adapt in a workplace where information and ideas can be shared directly through BCIs?

7.4 Ethical Considerations in the Workplace: Addressing Issues of Privacy and Mental Strain

The potential benefits of BCIs in the workplace are undeniable, but ethical considerations require careful attention:

- **Privacy and Security of Brain Data:** Robust safeguards are essential to protect employee brain data from unauthorized access and potential misuse.

- **Mental Strain and Workload Management:** Using BCIs for extended periods could lead to mental fatigue. It's crucial to establish clear guidelines and breaks to prevent work overload and ensure employee well-being.

- **Employee Autonomy and Coercion:** The use of BCIs in the workplace needs to be voluntary and not a requirement for employment. Employees should have control over how their brain data is used.

Conclusion

Brain-Computer Interfaces hold immense potential for transforming the workplace, from enhancing cognitive performance and optimizing skill development to facilitating seamless collaboration. However, alongside the excitement lies the responsibility to address ethical concerns and ensure responsible implementation. By prioritizing employee well-being, fostering open communication, and establishing clear ethical frameworks, BCIs can become a powerful tool for creating a more productive, efficient, and collaborative work environment. The future of work is rapidly evolving, and BCIs are poised to play a significant role in shaping that future.

CHAPTER 8

BCIs in National Defense and Security: Ethical Dilemmas in a Technological Age

Brain-Computer Interfaces (BCIs) hold immense potential for various applications, but their integration into national defense and security raises complex ethical dilemmas.

8.1 Brain-Computer Controlled Weapons: The Ethical Implications of Autonomous Warfare

One of the most concerning applications of BCIs in national defense is the possibility of brain-controlled weaponry. Imagine soldiers using their thoughts to directly fire weapons or control autonomous drones. This raises a multitude of ethical concerns:

- **The Removal of Human Decision-Making:** BCI-controlled weapons remove a critical element from warfare: human judgment. Life-or-death decisions made through the filter of human emotion and reason are replaced by the potentially dispassionate calculations of a machine.

- **The Risk of Accidental Escalation:** The speed and potential for misinterpretation of brain signals in the heat of combat could lead to accidental escalation of conflicts and unintended casualties.

- **The Blurring of Lines Between Combatant and Civilian:** With BCIs potentially controlling autonomous weapons, the distinction between combatants and civilians on the battlefield becomes increasingly blurred.

The development and deployment of BCI-controlled weapons pose a significant threat to global security and require a complete ban on such technologies.

8.2 Enhanced Soldier Performance: Ethical Considerations of Human Augmentation in the Military

BCIs could be used to enhance soldier performance in various ways:

- **Improved Situational Awareness:** Soldiers could receive real-time battlefield information and threat assessments directly through BCIs, enhancing their situational awareness and decision-making capabilities.

- **Augmented Physical Capabilities:** BCIs might one day be used to enhance a soldier's strength, endurance, or sensory perception on the battlefield.

- **Brain-Machine Interfaces for Prosthetic Control:** BCIs could allow for seamless control of advanced prosthetics, aiding wounded soldiers in returning to active duty.

Ethical Considerations of Human Augmentation:

While enhancing soldier performance offers advantages, ethical considerations need to be addressed:

- **The Long-Term Health Effects of BCI Implants:** The long-term health effects of implanting BCIs in soldiers' brains are not fully understood. Potential risks associated with brain-computer interfaces require thorough investigation.

- **The Commodification of Soldiers:** Does augmenting soldiers with BCIs turn them into mere tools of war, raising concerns about the dehumanization of warfare?

- **The Escalation of the Arms Race:** The development of BCI-enhanced soldiers could trigger a dangerous arms race between nations, leading to a constant push for more powerful and potentially more dangerous technologies.

The ethical implications of human augmentation in the military necessitate careful consideration and international dialogue.

8.3 Protecting National Security: Utilizing BCIs for Threat Detection and Intelligence Gathering

BCIs also hold potential benefits for national security beyond the battlefield:

- **Brain-Based Lie Detection:** While ethically contentious, BCIs might be used for interrogation purposes, attempting to detect deception through brain activity analysis. The reliability and accuracy of such methods remain highly debatable.

- **Enhanced Intelligence Gathering:** BCIs could potentially be used to analyze brain activity patterns of individuals suspected of terrorist activity or espionage, raising significant privacy concerns.

- **Protecting Critical Infrastructure:** BCIs could be used to monitor the brain activity of personnel guarding sensitive locations, potentially detecting signs of fatigue, distraction, or malicious intent.

The potential benefits of BCIs for national security must be weighed against the ethical implications of privacy violations, potential misuse of the technology, and the erosion of civil liberties.

8.4 The Quest for International Cooperation: Establishing Regulations for BCIs in Military Applications

The potential dangers of BCIs in warfare necessitate international cooperation to establish clear regulations and frameworks:

- **A Global Ban on Autonomous Weapons:** An

international treaty banning the development and deployment of autonomous weapons controlled by BCIs is crucial to prevent an arms race and safeguard human control over warfare.

- **Ethical Guidelines for Human Augmentation:** International guidelines are needed to ensure responsible development and use of BCIs for military purposes, focusing on soldier well-being, long-term health effects, and the avoidance of human augmentation that dehumanizes warfare.

- **International Oversight and Transparency:** Strong international oversight bodies are needed to monitor compliance with regulations and ensure responsible development and use of BCIs in national defense applications.

The future of BCIs in national defense hinges on

international cooperation and a commitment to ethical principles. Open dialogue, transparency, and a focus on global security are paramount to ensuring that this powerful technology is used responsibly and does not lead to a new era of devastating warfare.

BCIs offer a glimpse into a future where technology can enhance human capabilities in various domains. However, the integration of BCIs into national defense and security raises complex ethical dilemmas. The potential for autonomous weapons and the augmentation of soldiers with BCIs necessitates a global conversation about the responsible development and use of this technology.

International cooperation is crucial to establish clear regulations and frameworks that prioritize:

- **A ban on autonomous weapons controlled by BCIs:** Human judgment and decision-making must remain central to warfare.
- **Ethical guidelines for human augmentation:**

Soldier well-being, long-term health effects, and the avoidance of dehumanizing technologies require international consensus.

- **International oversight and transparency:** Strong oversight bodies are needed to monitor compliance with regulations and ensure responsible development and use of BCIs in national defense.

The future of BCIs in national defense hinges on a shared commitment to ethical principles. By prioritizing global security, fostering open dialogue, and ensuring responsible development, we can ensure that this powerful technology serves humanity and does not usher in a new era of devastating warfare.

Beyond national defense, the ethical considerations surrounding BCIs extend to other applications. Law enforcement, for instance, might explore using BCIs for suspect interrogation or lie detection. However, the potential for misuse and privacy violations raises significant concerns.

In conclusion, BCIs are a powerful and transformative technology with vast potential for positive applications. However, alongside the excitement lies the responsibility to address ethical challenges and ensure responsible development across all domains. Through open discussions, international collaboration, and a commitment to ethical principles, we can harness the power of BCIs to create a better future for all.

CHAPTER 9

THE PHILOSOPHICAL AND SOCIETAL IMPACT OF BCIs: RESHAPING HUMANITY

Brain-Computer Interfaces (BCIs) hold the potential to revolutionize not just how we interact with the world but also how we define ourselves.

9.1 Redefining What it Means to be Human: The Blurring of Man and Machine

As BCIs become more sophisticated, they raise fundamental questions about what it means to be human:

- **The Mind-Body Duality:** BCIs directly interface with the brain, the very essence of our being. Does augmentation with technology fundamentally alter our human identity?

- **The Nature of Consciousness:** If our thoughts and emotions can be influenced or augmented by technology, how do we define consciousness and free will?

- **The Blurring of Lines:** With BCIs seamlessly integrating with our brains, will the distinction between human and machine become increasingly blurred? Will we become a hybrid species, "cyborgs," with enhanced cognitive and physical capabilities?

These profound questions require ongoing philosophical and ethical discourse to guide the development and use of BCIs in a way that preserves what it means to be human.

9.2 The Quest for Transhumanism: Upgrading Ourselves Beyond Biological Limitations

Transhumanism is a philosophical movement that

advocates for the use of technology to overcome human limitations and enhance our physical, cognitive, and psychological capabilities. BCIs play a central role in this vision:

- **Augmenting Cognitive Abilities:** BCIs could allow us to think faster, learn more efficiently, and potentially even access information directly from the external world.

- **Enhancing Physical Capabilities:** BCIs might be used to control advanced prosthetics, interface with robotic exoskeletons, or even directly stimulate the nervous system to enhance physical performance.

- **Extending Lifespan:** BCIs could potentially play a role in future medical technologies aimed at treating neurological conditions, repairing brain damage, or even extending human lifespan.

However, the pursuit of transhumanism also raises concerns:

- **The Commodification of Enhancement:** Will BCI augmentation become a marker of social and economic status, exacerbating existing inequalities?

- **The Definition of "Natural":** If humans become increasingly reliant on technology for cognitive and physical enhancement, what remains of our natural state?

- **The Ethical Implications of Designer Babies:** Could BCIs pave the way for the manipulation of human traits and abilities even before birth, raising ethical concerns about designer babies and eugenics.

The potential benefits and drawbacks of transhumanism necessitate careful consideration and open dialogue to ensure responsible development and equitable access to

BCI augmentation technologies.

9.3 The Digital Divide: Ensuring Equitable Access to BCI Technology

The potential benefits of BCIs are vast, but ensuring equitable access is crucial to prevent the widening of the digital divide:

- **Socioeconomic Barriers:** The high cost of BCI development and implementation could create a situation where only the wealthy can afford BCI augmentation, exacerbating social inequalities.

- **Accessibility for People with Disabilities:** BCIs offer immense potential for enhancing the lives of people with disabilities. However, ensuring equitable access for all, regardless of socioeconomic background, is essential.

- **Global Development Considerations:** The benefits

of BCIs should not be limited to developed nations. International cooperation is needed to ensure equitable access for all countries.

Addressing the digital divide requires a multifaceted approach:

- **Government funding and research grants:** Public investment in BCI research and development can help drive down costs and make this technology more accessible.

- **Open-source development and collaboration:** Encouraging open-source development and international collaboration can accelerate innovation and make BCIs more affordable.

- **Ethical considerations in pricing models:** Developing ethical pricing models that balance innovation with affordability is essential for ensuring equitable access.

By prioritizing equitable access, we can ensure that the benefits of BCIs are not limited to a privileged few.

9.4 The Future of Consciousness: Exploring the Potential for Machine Consciousness

As BCIs become more sophisticated and AI advancements continue, the question of machine consciousness arises:

- **The Emergence of Artificial Consciousness:** Could BCIs one day play a role in the development of artificial general intelligence (AGI), potentially leading to machines that are conscious and self-aware?

- **The Nature of Subjectivity:** If machines can process information and respond to stimuli in ways that resemble human consciousness, how do we define the nature of subjectivity and sentience?

- **The Ethical Implications of Machine Consciousness:** If machines become conscious, what are the ethical implications for our relationship with them? Do they deserve rights and protections similar to those afforded to humans?

The possibility of machine consciousness presents a profound philosophical and ethical challenge. Open discourse and international collaboration are crucial to navigate these questions and ensure the responsible development of advanced AI.

Brain-Computer Interfaces stand at the precipice of a revolution, not just in technology, but in our very understanding of what it means to be human. From blurring the lines between man and machine to the quest for transhumanism and the potential for machine consciousness, BCIs raise profound philosophical and ethical questions.

As we move forward, it's crucial to prioritize responsible development, ensure equitable access, and engage in open discussions about the societal implications of this transformative technology. We must strive to harness the power of BCIs to enhance our lives, address inequalities, and navigate the ethical challenges that lie ahead. The future of BCIs is not simply technological; it's a conversation about the future of humanity itself.

By approaching BCI development with a spirit of collaboration, ethical responsibility, and a commitment to human well-being, we can ensure that this technology serves as a tool for progress, not a catalyst for division. The potential for BCIs to reshape humanity is undeniable, and the choices we make today will determine the course of this transformation for generations to come.

CHAPTER 10

THE ROAD AHEAD: NAVIGATING THE FUTURE OF BCIs

Brain-Computer Interfaces (BCIs) hold immense potential to revolutionize various aspects of our lives. However, navigating the path forward requires overcoming technical challenges, fostering open communication, establishing ethical frameworks, and embracing the vast untapped potential of this technology.

10.1 Overcoming Technical Challenges: Advancing Accuracy, Security, and Accessibility of BCIs

Despite the significant progress made, several technical challenges remain to be addressed:

- **Accuracy and Decoding Complexity:** Improving the accuracy and reliability of BCI systems in decoding complex brain activity patterns is crucial for a wider range of applications.

- **Security and Privacy Concerns:** Ensuring robust security measures to protect sensitive brain data from unauthorized access or manipulation is paramount.

- **Non-invasive and Implantable Technologies:** Developing safe, comfortable, and user-friendly non-invasive and implantable BCIs will be essential for wider adoption and long-term use.

- **Brain-Computer Interface Standardization:** Standardizing BCI interfaces and protocols will facilitate collaboration, accelerate innovation, and ensure compatibility between different systems.

Overcoming these challenges requires continued research and development efforts, focusing on:

- **Advanced machine learning algorithms:** Developing more sophisticated algorithms for decoding brain signals and improving the accuracy of BCIs.

- **Cybersecurity advancements:** Implementing robust cybersecurity measures to safeguard brain data privacy and prevent unauthorized access.

- **Biocompatible materials:** Developing safe and biocompatible materials for implantable BCIs to minimize health risks and improve user comfort.

- **Open-source collaboration:** Encouraging open-source collaboration and knowledge sharing among researchers and developers to accelerate BCI advancements.

By addressing these technical challenges, we can pave the

way for a future where BCIs are accurate, secure, accessible, and user-friendly.

10.2 The Role of Public Discourse: Fostering Open Communication About BCI Development

BCIs raise complex ethical and societal questions. Public discourse is essential to ensure responsible development and address potential concerns:

- **Open Discussions on Ethical Implications:** Open and transparent discussions about the ethical implications of BCIs, such as privacy concerns, human augmentation, and potential misuse, are crucial.

- **Public Education and Awareness:** Educating the public about the potential benefits and risks of BCIs empowers individuals to make informed decisions about their use.

- **Engaging with Diverse Stakeholders:** Including diverse stakeholders, including ethicists, neuroscientists, policymakers, and the public, in discussions about BCI development is necessary for a holistic approach.

Fostering open communication requires:

- **Public outreach programs:** Initiating public outreach programs to educate individuals about BCIs and encourage engagement in discussions about their development.

- **Independent oversight bodies:** Establishing independent oversight bodies to monitor BCI research and development, ensuring adherence to ethical principles.

- **Media engagement:** Engaging with media outlets to provide accurate and balanced information about

BCIs and foster public understanding.

By fostering open communication, we can build trust and ensure that BCIs are developed and used in a way that benefits society as a whole.

10.3 Building a Responsible Future: Ethical Frameworks for BCI Use and Development

The potential benefits of BCIs are vast, but ethical considerations require careful attention:

- **Informed Consent and User Control:** Robust informed consent procedures and mechanisms for user control over BCI data collection and use are essential.

- **Addressing Bias and Discrimination:** BCI algorithms and applications must be designed and tested to mitigate potential biases and prevent discrimination.

- **The Neuroethical Landscape:** Developing a robust neuroethical framework that guides research, development, and use of BCIs in a responsible and ethical manner is crucial.

Building a responsible future for BCIs requires:

- **International collaboration on ethical guidelines:** Developing international ethical guidelines for BCI research and development through collaboration between nations and scientific bodies.

- **Prioritizing transparency and accountability:** Ensuring transparency in BCI development and holding developers accountable for ethical violations.

- **Empowering individuals with knowledge:**

Empowering individuals with the knowledge and tools to make informed decisions about BCI use and protect their data privacy.

By prioritizing ethical principles and developing robust frameworks, we can ensure that BCIs are used responsibly and for the benefit of all.

10.4 A Look Towards the Horizon: The Untapped Potential of Brain-Computer Interfaces

BCIs are still in their early stages, but the potential applications are vast:

- **Brain-Machine Interfaces for Artistic Expression:** BCIs could allow artists to directly translate their thoughts and emotions into creative works, opening doors to new artistic frontiers.
- **Enhanced Learning and Education:** BCIs could personalize learning experiences, improve

information retention, and revolutionize the education sector by tailoring instruction to individual needs and cognitive styles.

- **Brain-Based Rehabilitation:** BCIs hold immense promise for rehabilitation after strokes, spinal cord injuries, and other neurological conditions, offering patients new avenues for regaining control and improving their quality of life.

- **Augmented Reality and Virtual Reality Integration:** BCIs could seamlessly integrate with AR and VR environments, creating immersive experiences that directly stimulate the brain and push the boundaries of human perception.

- **The Future of Brain-Computer Interfaces and Artificial Intelligence:** The convergence of BCIs and AI could lead to groundbreaking advancements in artificial general intelligence (AGI), potentially fostering a future where humans and machines collaborate on an even deeper level.

However, exploring these possibilities requires careful consideration of potential risks:

- **The Digital Divide and Equity of Access:** Ensuring equitable access to BCI technology for all socioeconomic backgrounds is crucial to prevent the exacerbation of existing inequalities.

- **The Potential for Addiction and Cognitive Overload:** The immersive nature of BCIs raises concerns about potential addiction and the need for responsible use to avoid cognitive overload.

- **The Unforeseen Consequences of Brain Augmentation:** The long-term effects of brain augmentation with BCIs are still unknown, and careful research is needed to mitigate potential risks.

As we explore the vast potential of BCIs, we must prioritize:

- **Sustainable development practices:** Developing BCIs in a sustainable and environmentally conscious manner to minimize the environmental footprint of this technology.

- **Global collaboration and knowledge sharing:** Fostering international collaboration and knowledge sharing among researchers and developers to accelerate advancements and ensure responsible development.

- **A human-centered approach:** Ensuring that BCI development remains focused on human well-being, empowerment, and the augmentation of our capabilities without compromising what it means to be human.

The future of BCIs is brimming with possibilities. By addressing technical challenges, fostering open communication, building a responsible framework, and approaching this technology with a spirit of collaboration and ethical responsibility, we can harness the power of BCIs to create a brighter future for all. BCIs are not just about technological advancements; they represent a chance to redefine our relationship with technology, reshape our understanding of ourselves, and push the boundaries of human potential. The journey ahead is one of exploration, discovery, and responsible innovation. As we embark on this path, it is with the hope that BCIs will serve not to divide us, but to unite us in a shared pursuit of a better future for humanity.

ABOUT THE AUTHOR

Writer's Bio:

 Benjamin Evans, a respected figure in the tech world, is known for his insightful commentary and analysis. With a strong educational background likely in fields such as computer science, engineering, or business, he brings a depth of knowledge to his discussions on emerging technologies and industry trends. Evans' knack for simplifying complex concepts, coupled with his innate curiosity and passion for innovation, has established him as a go-to source for understanding the dynamics of the digital landscape. Through articles, speeches, and social media, he shares his expertise and offers valuable insights into the impact of technology on society.

www.ingramcontent.com/pod-product-compliance
Lightning Source LLC
LaVergne TN
LVHW051701050326
832903LV00032B/3944